Reading
and
Language
Skills Book

When you see this symbol it means you will need a copy of the book.

Heinemann

Contents

Short Stories

Peacemaker and Other Stories

Plays

The Pardoner's Tale and Other Plays

Cal's Crossword

Crosswords have different types of clues:

- general knowledge clues
- anagrams – letters which are mixed up *e.g. march – charm*
- words which sound like or rhyme with those in the clue *e.g. ham – jam*

A Copy this crossword and fill in the answers to the clues.

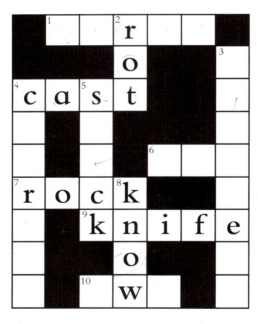

ACROSS

1 The symbol Cal makes on the rock walls. (5)

6 An anagram of Pam. (3)

10 Mac and Anna are _____ children. (3)

DOWN

3 An adjective which describes the ledge Anna and Mac had to cross. (8)

4 Another word for bravery. (7)

5 Sounds like track. (5)

B 1 Draw a grid, 7 squares by 9 squares, like the one above.

2 Design your own crossword and clues, choosing your own theme. Use a dictionary and thesaurus to help you.

Prefixes, Suffixes and Roots

> The root is the main part of a word.
> Prefixes are joined on to the beginning of a word.
> Suffixes are added to the end of a word. *e.g. en joy ment*
>
> prefix   root   suffix

A Open the story of *Cal's Log* at any full page of text. Write as many words as you can find which have more than five letters **and** have a root within them. Underline the root.

e.g. *turned, bravely, somehow, important*

B Work with a partner.

1 Each think of a word that describes an emotion Mac or Anna felt during the story, *e.g. joy*.

2 Tell your partner your word, for him or her to write down.

3 Give yourselves seven minutes. Draw a spider diagram, with the root word in the centre. Add words around it by adding prefixes and/or suffixes to the root word.

e.g.

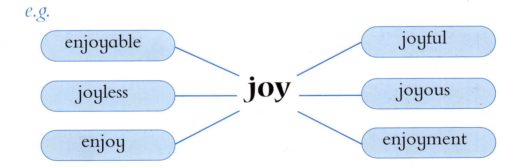

4 Swap diagrams. Using a dictionary, check the spelling of your partner's words. Who has the most words spelt correctly?

Simile and Metaphor

A simile is when one thing is said to be similar to another, using the words 'as' and 'like'. *e.g. The cliffs were like an angry giant.*

A metaphor is when one thing is described as if it were something else. *e.g. the angry giant cliffs*

The simile is comparing the cliffs to an angry giant. This tells us that the cliffs are huge. Maybe they look 'angry' because there are lots of crevices in the cliff face.

A 1 Re-read pages 6-7 of *Cal's Log*.

2 Write one simile from these pages.

3 Explain what the simile tells you.

B 1 Re-read page 10.

2 Write down five suggestions for how the author could add a simile or metaphor to this page. Write whether your suggestion is a simile or a metaphor.

> e.g. *The glow disappeared like ... a candle being snuffed out. (simile)*
> *The sky turned ... ink black. (metaphor)*

Ideas to help you:
The storm broke overhead like ...
The weather had turned in seconds, like ...

Types of Texts

Reports tell you about facts. *e.g. newspaper reports*

Persuasive texts try to persuade you to do or buy something. *e.g. brochures*

Recounts describe personal experiences. *e.g. diaries*

Instructional texts explain how something is done. *e.g. instruction manuals*

A 1 Read the writing on each of the torn pieces of paper. Each is based on the setting, characters or events in *Cal's Log*. Write which type of text you think each is.

a **Come and visit** the wonderful island of Shetland. See its

b
> 1. Take out the flare.
> 2. Strike a match.

c
> Two children had a close escape from death when

d
> Time of rescue:
> 19:00 hrs
>
> Details of rescue:
> Two children were

e
> When Mac and I set out I did feel a little nervous, but

2 Write who you think wrote each extract. *e.g. d) police officer*

B Choose one of the text extracts. Continue it in your own words.

Think about:
- the kind of layout your text type should have
- the kind of language your text type should use

Try to find other examples of this type of text to help you.

Investigating Language

A Re-read Cal's first diary entry on pages 24-27 of *Cal's Log*. List all the objects or people Cal mentions which give us clues that the story is set in the past.

B Cal's entry is written in a more formal style than we use today. Copy each of Cal's thoughts below on a new line. Beside each thought write how Cal would express his thoughts if he were writing today.

Ideas to help you:

• Could you use contractions? *e.g. could not – couldn't*
• Could you miss out some words?
• Do you need to change the words, or change their order?

1 I fear I must leave you soon.

(page 49)

2 Honour my name, I beg you.

(page 49)

3 Checking the map has weakened me still further.

(page 48)

4 If you discover my corpse tell my father about me and what has happened.

(page 49)

C List words which people used in the past, but which we do not use today. You can look through a Bible or a book written a long time ago to help you. Try to find out their meanings.

Complex Sentences

Complex sentences have more than one clause. (A clause is a group of words which has a verb. *e.g. I've dropped the torch.*) The clauses in complex sentences are joined by connectives *e.g. and, but, then, because, when, so, after, until.* Each clause makes sense on its own.
e.g. The sun broke through the clouds and the wind lessened.

1st clause   connective   2nd clause

A Read each sentence. List all the connectives from the box above which would make sense where the star appears.

1 Mac could not stop. ☆ The current swept him past Anna.

2 Panic had gripped them both now. ☆ The gusts began to get harder, more vicious.

B Work with a partner.

1 Find four connectives in this passage.

2 Take it in turns to read the passage. One person reads it with the connectives, the other without.

3 Write which version you think gets across the terror and tension of the situation. Try to explain why.

    There was no guarantee they would find an escape route, and another tunnel might lead them back into the centre.
    The dangers blazed in Mac and Anna's minds as they gazed down at the surging swell.
    Mac was already moving away from Anna and she grabbed his wrist, pulling him back. Mac had never felt so afraid in his life and his mouth was so dry he just couldn't argue any more.

Comparing Problems and Solutions

In *Cal's Log* Anna and Mac have to try to find their way out of the stack. Along the way they encounter many problems and have to find ways to solve them.

A These pictures show some of the problems the children encounter. Write each problem and explain how the children solve each of them. Use the page numbers to help you.

1 (pages 14–15)

2 (page 18)

3 (pages 21–22)

4 (pages 38–40)

5 (pages 61–63)

B List the titles of any other stories you have read where the main characters have to find something or save someone. Write a few sentences to say what problems they encounter and solve along the way.

Writing a Review

A You are going to write a review of *Cal's Log* for other people in your class to read.

1 List the things you would want to read in a book review.

e.g. the genre (type of story)

adventure?   historical?

the characters

important events

author

The sea was flat and calm with a strange glow

publisher

2 Write your review of *Cal's Log* by Anthony Masters.

Ideas to think about:
- What headings will you use?
- How will you present written information? *e.g. lists, quotes, speech bubbles*
- Where will you use pictures?
- What kind of information will you include to make your reader want to read the book?

Remember not to give away the ending!

Flashbacks

> Throughout the story of *Cal's Log* we move between being with Mac and Anna to reading extracts from Cal's diary. Going back in time in a story is called a flashback.

A 1 Re-read the last three paragraphs on page 30 and the first two on page 31. In what ways are Mac's and Cal's experiences similar? Write your ideas.

2 Re-read pages 45-47. In what ways are Cal's experiences similar to or different from Mac's and Anna's experiences in this section of the story? Write your ideas.

B Re-read the last chapter, pages 79-80, and Cal's first diary entry on pages 24-27. Imagine you are Cal's father. Write a paragraph from his diary on the day that he was given the news that Cal's ship had sunk.

Think about:
- what Cal's father knew about why the ship sank
- where the ship sank
- what job Cal was doing on board
- how his father would have felt when he found out about his son

C You have now written a flashback. Where do you think it would fit best into the story? At the beginning, middle or end? Explain the reason for your choice.

Cool Cues

> **Cues** are one way you can help yourself learn and remember spellings.
> *e.g. finding little words in big words*
>   <u>bus</u>iness   <u>ghost</u>   <u>fri</u>end
> *e.g. splitting a word into syllables*
>   Wed/nes/day   tem/per
> *e.g. saying out loud any silent letters*
>   <u>k</u>night   lam<u>b</u>

A Scrooge from *A Christmas Carol* wants to find ways to help Tiny Tim remember these spellings.

1 Write each word and next to it write the best cue to help Tiny Tim remember the spelling.

    a humour   **e** glistened

    b knocker   **f** bygone

    c phantom   **g** length

    d solitary

2 Work with a partner. Take it in turns to read out each word and a cue for it. The other person writes that word. The reader of the cue checks the writer's spelling.

B Work together to find other words in the story which Tiny Tim may find difficult to spell. Write some cues for the words to help him.

Changing Language

A 1 Read this passage from the end of *A Christmas Carol* when Scrooge discovers he is back in his own bed.

> *But now he was so flustered … that he was for a minute all a'twitter. 'I don't know what to do!' he said … 'I am as light as a feather, I am as happy as an angel, I am as merry as a schoolboy! A Merry Christmas to everyone …'* (page 72)

    2 Write what you think the word **'a'twitter'** means.

    3 Think of words that we use today which are similar.

B Think of modern comparisons to complete Scrooge's similes.

    1 I am as light as …

    2 I am as happy as …

    3 I am as merry as …

C 1 Scan through the story. Find six words we do not use today or whose meaning has changed and write them down.
e.g. counting-house (page 4)

    2 Write what you think each word means. Then compare your meanings with those in a dictionary.

Stressed Words

A Write the following list of words. Read each word aloud.
Underline the part of the word you stress or say most strongly.
e.g. <u>Hum</u>bug!

1	shiver	**5**	haunted
2	spectre	**6**	ghostly
3	dismal	**7**	despair
4	misery	**8**	gloomy

B In films like 'Star Wars', there are computers which pronounce
every syllable and have no stresses in their words. It might sound
boring to speak like this, but it can help you to learn to spell
words.

1 Write the following words as if
a computer were saying them.
e.g. mystery: mys – ter – y

    a gentleman   **d** spirit

    b transparent   **e** invisible

    c apparition   **f** convenient

2 Work with a partner and test each
other on these spellings.

Hello

Spot the Difference

Dickens' version

Oh! but he was a tight-fisted hand at the grindstone, Scrooge! A squeezing, wrenching, grasping, scraping, clutching, covetous old sinner! Hard and sharp as flint, from which no steel had ever struck out generous fire; secret, and self contained, and solitary as an oyster.

Adaptation by M Lawrence

Oh, but Scrooge was a tight-fisted, squeezing, wrenching, clutching, grasping old sinner! Hard and sharp as flint, he was, and secretive and solitary as an oyster.

A Make a list of five changes which Michael Lawrence made when he adapted Dickens' description of Scrooge.
These could be:

- changes in punctuation
  e.g. Mr Lawrence doesn't use an '!' after 'Oh'
- different vocabulary
- sections of text left out

B List some things you know about Scrooge from Dickens' description which you would not know from reading Michael Lawrence's description. You can use a dictionary to check the meaning of any words you don't know.

C Which description of Scrooge do you prefer and why?

Cracking Colons and Semi-colons

Colons (:) are used:
- before a list
  e.g. *In front of him were the following*: *mince pies, holly and other delicious delights.*
- to link two clauses, when the second one gives more information about the first.
  e.g. *Around its middle the chain was clasped*: *long, and wound about him like a tail.*

A Find the colon on each of these pages and write whether it is used before a list, or to link two clauses.

1 (page 3)   2 (page 42)   3 (page 57)   4 (page 64)

Semi-colons (;) are used:
- to separate longer items in a list
  e.g. *There were snowflakes falling*; *there were children shouting*; *the wind was dancing.*
- to link two clauses, which are closely related.
  e.g. *He knew these boys, everyone*; *could name them all.*

B Find the semi-colon on each of these pages and write whether it is used to separate longer items in a list, or to link two clauses.

1 (page 12)   2 (page 24)   3 (page 37)   4 (page 49)

Connectives Competition

> **Connectives** are words which join sentences or clauses together. *e.g. and, but, yet, also, because, so, until, then*

A 1   Work with a partner. Each open *A Christmas Carol* on a different page. Write all the connectives which appear on your page. Who has found the most connectives?

    2   With your partner, look up in a thesaurus three of the connectives you have found. Use the thesaurus to add as many other connectives to your list as you can.

B Work with your partner. Re-tell a story you both know well, *e.g. Cinderella*. One person starts the story, saying a sentence, and finishes with a connective.

e.g. Cinderella lived with her two sisters who …

The other person says another clause, also ending in a connective.

e.g. … were extremely ugly and …

Continue in the same way until you reach the end of the story.

Dickens' Descriptions

A Read this passage from page 4 of *A Christmas Carol*.

It was cold, bleak, biting weather, and he could hear the people outside wheezing by, beating their hands upon their chests and stamping their feet upon the pavement to warm them. The city clocks had only just gone three, but it was quite dark already, and candles flared in the windows of neighbouring offices. Fog came pouring in at every chink and keyhole, and was so dense outside that the houses opposite were mere phantoms.

B 1 Write any words you do not understand. Find the words in a dictionary and write their meanings.

2 The passage is a description written to make you feel what it was like to be there. Copy the table, listing words or phrases from the passage which describe:

sounds	darkness/death	temperature/weather

C Write your own description of an eerie place, in the style of Dickens.
e.g. a foggy city, snow-covered moors, haunted ruins at night

A Christmas Carol Quiz

A Write answers to these quiz questions. Try to answer the questions without looking back at the story.

> **1** Fill in the missing word.
> *'He then put on his dressing gown and his slippers and his _____ ...'*
>
> **2** Which character says this?
> *'I come tonight to warn you, Ebenezer ...'*
>
> **3** Describe one thing about the appearance of the second ghost.
>
> **4** Name three children who are mentioned in the story.
>
> **5** True or False?
> *Scrooge was taken by the Ghost of Christmas Present to a lighthouse.*

Check your answers on the following pages:
1 (page 11), **2** (page 15), **3** (page 36), **4** (page 41), **5** (page 46)

B Write five quiz questions about *A Christmas Carol* for a partner to answer. Try to use a range of questions.
e.g. Fill in the missing word.
  List three things.
  Which character says this?
  True or false?

Writing a Play

A 1 Re-read from 'They went on, invisibly ...' on page 38 of
A Christmas Carol, to '... growing strong and hearty'
on page 40.

2 Make a list of the characters who appear in this scene. Explain
who each character is – his or her approximate age and
appearance.

3 Describe where the scene is taking place – the decoration, the
furniture, the time of day. Explain what happens before Mrs
Cratchit speaks on page 38.

4 Write pages 38–40 as a play. Include a narrator and stage
directions. You could set out your play like this.

A Christmas Carol (Pages 38–40)

Mrs Cratchit: *(looking out of the window) Wherever has
your father got to?*

Mnemonic Fun

> **Mnemonics** help you remember how to spell words.
> Write a saying, starting with each letter, for the difficult part
> of the word.
> e.g. **b** **e** **a** **u** tiful – **b**ig **e**lephants **a**re **u**gly

A 1 Write out mnemonics for the following words. Concentrate on
the part of the word you find hard to remember.

   a budgie *e.g. b* ＿＿＿ *u* ＿＿＿ *d* ＿＿＿ *g* ＿＿＿ *i* ＿＿＿ *e* ＿＿＿

   b bomber

   c sirens

   d aching

   e dial

  2 Swap your ideas with a friend and test each other on the
spelling of each word.

B Look through the story *Under the Bomber's Moon* and find five
words that are not easy to spell. Make up mnemonics to help you
learn them.

22

Police Summary

Imagine you are one of the police officers who helped to rescue David, Max and Mr Potter in *Under the Bomber's Moon*.

A 1 Re-read the events surrounding the rescue on pages 19–20.

2 Fill in a report of the rescue for your commanding officer in the Greater Manchester police force. Use the headings on the Incident Report Form to help you. You may need to read back through the story to fill in the details.

Things to think about before you start:
- What style of writing will you use to write the report? Formal? Informal? Notes or full sentences?

GREATER MANCHESTER POLICE

INCIDENT REPORT

Time: _____ Place: _____

Names of people involved: _____

_____

Summary (in no more than 30 words) _____

_____

_____

_____

Signature of reporting police officer _____

Action Verbs

A 1 Re-read pages 14–15.

   2 Find nine verbs to do with action. You could set out your work in a spider diagram like this.

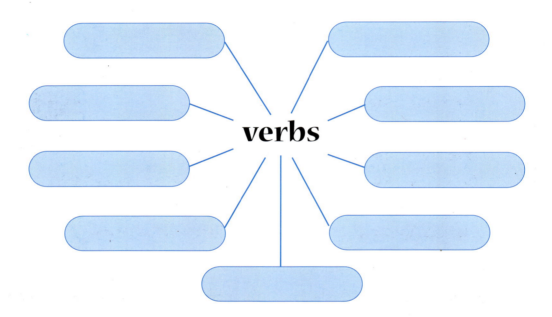

   3 List three verbs you have found that best describe the chaos that surrounds David.

B Write your own description of a bomb exploding, using powerful verbs.

   Ideas to think about:
- the sounds the bomb will make
- the actions of people *e.g. panicking/running/shouting*
- the effect of the bomb on the surrounding buildings and objects *e.g. glass windows, cars*

Clause Challenge

A **clause** is a group of words with a verb (action word) in it.
e.g. Peter **told** his mother about Albert.
A **complex sentence** has a **main clause** and a **subordinate clause**. The subordinate clause does not make sense on its own.
e.g. <u>Peter looked inside the bag</u> *and* <u>thanked his mum.</u>

        ▲   ▲   ▲
    main clause   connective subordinate clause

A 1 Re-read pages 35–37 of *Albert*. Find a sentence with one clause and write it down.

  2 Find a sentence with one main and one subordinate clause. Write the sentence and label the main clause and the subordinate clause.

  3 Find a sentence which has a main clause and two subordinate clauses. Write the sentence and label the clauses.

Sometimes you can change the order of the clauses, putting the subordinate clause first. *e.g.*

<u>*So that he could attend to some business*</u>, <u>*John Harper walked back with his wife.*</u>

                ↑   ↑
        subordinate clause   main clause

B Re-write these sentences, putting the subordinate clause first. You may have to change the order of the words, or add words of your own.

  1 The fire was put out with John Harper's help.

  2 The ears of wheat were left to stand and dry out in the sun before they were carted off and built into stacks.

Developing Characters

In *Albert* two characters from opposite sides find out about, and learn to trust each other. It is the Second World War and Britain and Germany are at war. Peter is British, Albert is a German prisoner of war.

A Write the answers to these questions.

   1 What does Peter think of Germans before he meets Albert? (page 32)

   2 What things does Albert do which makes Peter see him as a person rather than a German enemy? (pages 32-34)

   3 What two things does Peter do which make Albert trust him? (pages 36-37; page 43)

B Think of other situations in which the characters could be on different sides but learn about and grow to trust each other. Make a list of characters who could be on opposite sides at the beginning of a story. Use these pictures to help you.

C List any stories you have read, or films you have seen, in which the characters are on opposite sides. How do they learn to trust each other?

Words to Win an Argument

A Re-read pages 48, 53 and 60 of *Alf the Spycatcher*.

1 List two things that Alf finds out about Mr Kolenski that convinces him Mr Kolenski is a spy.

2 Imagine you are Alf. Write down what you will say to convince Captain Harding that Mr Kolenski is a spy. Try to include some of these words or phrases.
   - *I believe …*
   - *I have found that …*
   - *This evidence shows …*
   - *Therefore …*
   - *Whereas …*
   - *This leads me to conclude …*

B Write down other useful words or phrases, like those in the lists above, which you could use to help you link your points together in an argument.

Sources of ideas to help you:
   - letters to the editor in a newspaper
   - campaign leaflet

HIGHTOWN BYPASS

As you can see, this evidence shows …

Letters to the Editor

Dear Sir,

I am writing to draw your attention to something which I believe …

Analysing Alf

A 1   Read these sentences about Alf.

a   'Don't make a sound,' said Alf. 'Mr Kolenski's gone out. I'm going to follow him.' (page 63)

b   Alf recognised … a German Luger pistol. He'd seen them often enough in his comics. (page 69)

c   His mum gave Alf a half shake, half hug. Alf found himself shivering for some reason and hugged her back. (page 74)

d   Vera gazed at her brother confidently. 'What shall we do next, Alf?' (page 61)

e   Alf wondered whether Captain Harding had only been pretending to take him seriously. Grown-ups were always doing that. (page 59)

2   Explain what each quote tells you about Alf.

Ideas to think about:
- how he feels
- his likes and dislikes
- his personality
- how others see him

B Write your opinion of Alf. Do you think he was brave? Why?

Summarizing a Chapter

Chapter titles give clues about each chapter, using as few words as possible.

A 1 Read these chapter titles from the story *Under the Bomber's Moon*.

Chapter 1
Bad news from London

Chapter 2
Bedtime escape

Chapter 3
Night on fire

Chapter 4
The bomb

2 Copy each chapter title. Beside each title write either a) or b) to show which statement best describes it.

a) describing an event that will happen
b) introducing an important subject

B 1 Remind yourself of the main events in Chapter 1 of *The Minefield* by re-reading pages 78-80 and write a short chapter title.

2 Write a chapter title for each of the other chapters. Write briefly why you chose each title.

Your Reaction

A 1   Read this passage from *The Minefield* when Rikki, Alen's dog, is killed.

> 'Rikki!' shouted Alen. 'Rikki! Get up! Come back!'
> There was no response from the dog.
> Alen ran to the edge of the field. Ilma also began to run. 'No, Alen!' she called desperately. 'Wait!' But he could not hear her. He scrambled through the gap in the hedge and shouted again to his dog. Rikki raised his head from the ground and gave a desolate whimper, a cry for help. Alen immediately set off towards him. Ilma ran as hard as she could but the way to the field was uphill. There was cold fear in her throat and her breath came in sobs. For the moment the hedge hid Alen from her view.
> Then she heard the second thud of an exploding mine. Now the fear clutched her heart and she groaned with despair. 'Alen!'

2   List the words and phrases from the passage that show how Ilma and Alen feel.

3   Write all the verbs (action words) used in the passage which show the speed at which the action is happening.

4   What do the exclamation marks (!) in this passage tell you about how the direct speech should be said?

B How do you feel when you read this passage? Give as many reasons as you can for your answer.

'i' and 'e'

There are three easy rules to help you remember how to spell words with 'i' and 'e' following each other.

A Teacher Faber in *Peacemaker* gives Michela these words to spell.

1 Make a list of all the words in which **i** and **e** together make the sound 'ee', *e.g. brief*. Do not use any words where the two letters come straight after the letter 'c'. What do you notice about the order of **i** and **e** in these words?

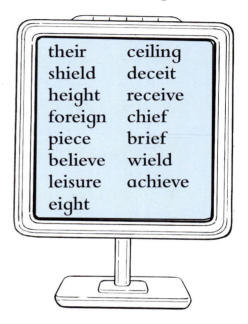

their	ceiling
shield	deceit
height	receive
foreign	chief
piece	brief
believe	wield
leisure	achieve
eight	

2 List all the words where **e** and **i** come straight after the letter 'c', *e.g. deceit*. Which order do **e** and **i** always come in, following straight after the letter 'c'?

3 List the words where **i** and **e** together don't make the sound 'ee', *e.g. eight*. What order do **i** and **e** always come in when their sound is not 'ee'?

B Help Michela learn the spelling rule by writing the missing letters from Teacher Faber's rule book.

> **i** comes before **e** when the sound is _____ **except** after the letter ____

Formal, Official Language

A Work with a partner. One of you will be Captain Corbin and the other is Fflqa-Tur from *Peacemaker*.

1   Read aloud what Captain Corbin and Fflqa-Tur say to each other from page 12 when Captain Corbin says 'Ensign Natsua …' to when she commands 'Comms down …' on page 15. They both use formal, official language.

2   Write the speech in the speech bubbles below, then change the language so that it is informal. What effect does it have when you change the words Captain Corbin and Fflqa-Tur use?
    e.g. This is Captain Corbin – 'Hi, I'm Captain Corbin.'

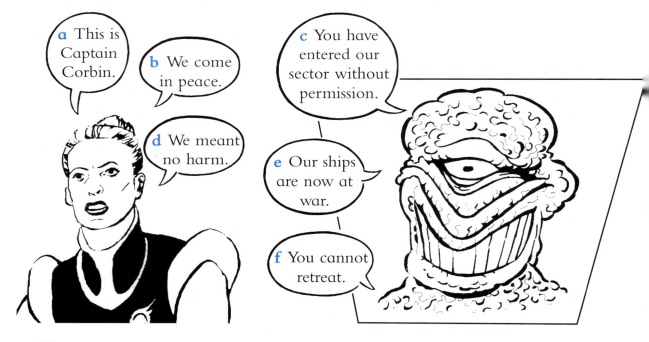

a This is Captain Corbin.

b We come in peace.

c You have entered our sector without permission.

d We meant no harm.

e Our ships are now at war.

f You cannot retreat.

B Imagine you are the captain of a spacecraft.

1   Write a greeting you would give to all alien spacecraft, in three or four sentences. Try to use formal, official language.

2   Read your greeting aloud to a partner, and listen to their greeting.

A Tense Battle

A 1 Read this description of Michela's dramatic fight with Fflqa-Tur from page 26 of *Peacemaker*.

> *Fflqa-Tur stepped into the arena. The crowd around us fell into an expectant silence … Flfqa-Tur raised his weapon and started moving towards me. Immediately, instinctively, I backed away, raising my sword between us. Fflqa-Tur and I circled warily around each other. My heart was about to explode from my chest. I could hear the blood roaring and rushing in my ears like a stormy sea. Fflqa-Tur lunged at me. Too terrified to even cry out, I leapt back.*

   2 You have been asked to make a tape of sound effects, to add tension to a reading of the passage. For each sentence list the sound effect you would record, and how you would make it. Set out your work like this.

Sentence	Sound effect	Object/Person needed to make it
1		
2		

Ideas to think about:
- Could you use musical instruments or parts of the body?
- Are there sentences when absolute silence would be best?
- Are there sentences when there could be many sounds at the same time?

B 1 Re-read page 28, from the line 'Heart pounding …' to the end of the page.

   2 List the five main sound effects you would use for this passage.

Is it Murder?

A 1 Re-read the final paragraph on page 44 of *One is One and All Alone*.

2 List the reasons why Trish wants to kill Clo.

B 1 Read this extract in which Trish thinks about whether or not to dispose of Clo.

> *Well, it wouldn't be murder, would it? How could it be? You can't be charged with murdering yourself, can you? You couldn't even be charged with suicide, because there will still be a person left …* (page 46)

2 Imagine you are Trish, lying in bed that night. Write down all the other reasons you can think of both for and against killing Clo. Write each thought inside a thought bubble.

Ideas for words to help you:
if, then, might, perhaps, could, would

Computer Speak

A On pages 36–37 of *One is One and All Alone* Trish has a conversation with VP the computer. Read these quotes from these pages and write whether Trish or VP is speaking.

> **1** WE MUST BE PATIENT. FOR NOW, I AM YOUR TRUE FRIEND.
>
> **2** GREAT. RIGHT, HERE I COME, THROUGH THE SMOKE … TWO, THREE, FOUR – ACTION …
>
> **3** NO, LET'S NOT PLAY ANY MORE. TEACH ME SOMETHING.
>
> **4** WE REACHED 'CLO'. SO I TAUGHT YOU ABOUT CLOCKS.
>
> **5** TEACH ME ABOUT CLONES AND CLONING, THEN.

B Work with a partner. One of you will act as VP, and the other will be Trish. Write a conversation between VP and Trish. They are speaking to each other the day after Clo has dumped Trish in the disposal hatch.

Ideas for questions:

VP questioning Trish
- What did you do last night, Trish?
- What do you want to know about today?
- Are you unhappy about being on your own?

Trish questioning VP
- How long until we get to Trion?
- What would happen if someone fell out of the disposal hatch?
- Do you think it is right to clone animals and people, VP?

Simple Spelling

Joel from *Rehearsal* has to pass a spelling exam so that he can go to St Theodore's School. The virtual future machine shows two ways to help him learn his spellings. These are called cues.

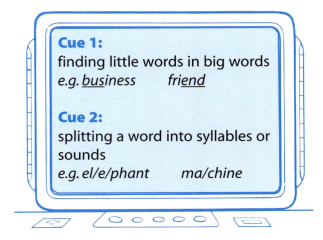

Cue 1:
finding little words in big words
e.g. <u>bus</u>iness   fri<u>end</u>

Cue 2:
splitting a word into syllables or sounds
e.g. el/e/phant   ma/chine

A Write each word and choose a cue to show how Joel can learn the spelling of the word.
e.g. popular – I can find a little word - pop<u>ular</u>

1 popular   3 virtual   5 excited
2 predicted   4 interested   6 realistic

B Work with a partner. Take it in turns to read out each word and a cue. The other person writes the word. The reader then checks whether the writer has spelt the word correctly.

C Write these words filling in the missing letters with those given by the virtual future machine.

1 su__ess
2 s__olarship
3 int__rested
4 re__listic
5 w__irred

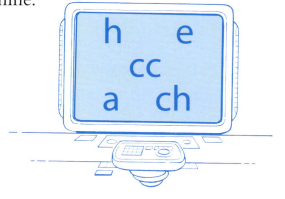

h   e
cc
a   ch

Time Machine

A 1 Re-read page 56 and the top of page 57 of *Rehearsal* in which Joel tries to learn how to become a famous footballer.

2 Children's TV is going to make a film about Joel's adventures on the virtual future machine. However, when the director is carrying the papers showing the order of events, she drops them. List the correct order of events.
Set out your work like this: **1d 2 3 4 5 6 7**

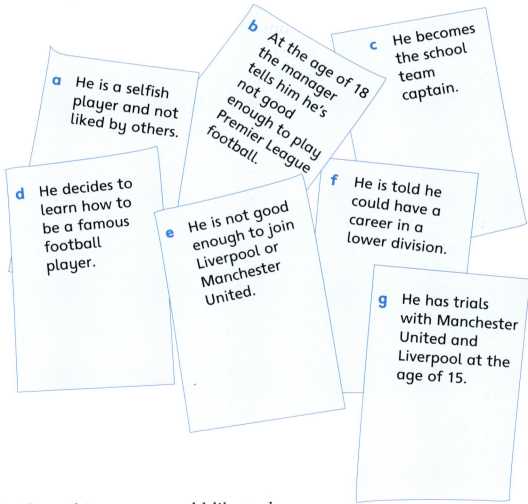

a He is a selfish player and not liked by others.

b At the age of 18 the manager tells him he's not good enough to play Premier League football.

c He becomes the school team captain.

d He decides to learn how to be a famous football player.

e He is not good enough to join Liverpool or Manchester United.

f He is told he could have a career in a lower division.

g He has trials with Manchester United and Liverpool at the age of 15.

B List three things you would like to happen in your life in the future, and give reasons why.

Note Making

Trust Me is being made into a play. Scott cannot remember the order of the events in the kitchen when he gets up in the night for a drink.

A 1 Re-read the first three paragraphs on page 73.

2 List the eight things Scott must remember to do in the correct order.

a creep down stairs

b _____

c _____

d _____

e _____

f _____

g _____

h _____

B 1 Read the following extract from page 76.

> *Scott stood up and went over to the cupboard for a tin of cat food. He got the opener out of the cutlery drawer and started opening the tin … Scott sensed a sharp pain in his finger as the tin skated away from him and fell to the floor. Shackleton leapt in fright and shot off under the table, bumping against a leg.*

2 List all the things that happen to Scott and Shackleton in the scene. List the events in the order they happen.

Scott   **Shackleton**

  a   e

  b   f

  c   g

  d

Science Fiction Stories

A List the typical ingredients in science fiction stories. Think about science fiction books, films and television programmes you may have read or seen, *e.g. Star Wars, E.T.*

Think about:
- characters *e.g. beings from other planets, spacecraft commander*
- places and time *e.g. inside a flying saucer, in the future*
- events *e.g. time travel, stranded on a strange planet*

B 1 Read this passage from the start of *Trust Me* on page 67.

Scott had been trying to get to sleep for ages when he heard a car stop in the quiet street outside. He lay rigid and listened to muffled voices, the car moving off, footsteps coming up the path.

2 The author wants to use the same opening paragraph, but change what happens next. He is looking for ideas. Use your imagination and the list you made in section A to think of as many ideas as you can.

Questions to think about:
- What vehicle might have sounded like a car stopping outside the house?
- Who might the people have been, talking in muffled voices? What might they have been talking about?
- Why did the vehicle leave?
- Who or what could have been coming up the path?

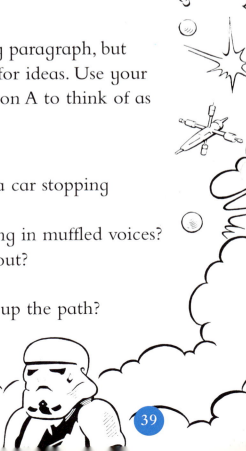

Skilful Spelling

A Each of the words below from *The Pardoner's Tale* can be difficult to spell correctly.

1 Work with a partner. Take it in turns to read the words. (Read what you think each word would be if it were complete.)

a vill_ _n   **f** d_saster

b miser_ble   **g** ex_austed

c just_ce   **h** sil_nce

d happ_ness   **i** rog_e

e inten_ion   **j** furi_ _s

2 On your own, write how you think each word is spelt.

3 Mark each other's work, using a dictionary to help you check the spelling.

B Work together. Go back through each of the words you spelt in section A. Take it in turns to say a sentence using one of the words. You could talk about the characters, the places or the events in the play.

> Ace was the real villain in the play.

40

Active and Passive Verbs

Verbs (action words) are active when the subject of the sentence does the action.

e.g. *The Pardoner told the tale.*

　　　▲　　　　▲
　subject　active verb

Verbs are passive when the subject of the sentence has the action done to it.

e.g. *The tale was told by the Pardoner.*

　　　▲　　　▲
　subject　passive verb

A Re-write these sentences changing the verb from active to passive.

　e.g. People filled the Inn. (Active)
　The Inn was filled with people. (Passive)

1　The Pardoner <u>told</u> his tale.

2　The hooligans <u>pushed</u> the old man.

3　The chemist <u>gave</u> Jack a bottle.

B Re-write these sentences changing the verb from passive to active.

1　The shopping was done by Jack.

2　The ruffians were amazed by the huge pile of money.

3　The old man was pushed out of the way by the three hooligans.

C Look through another play in *The Pardoner's Tale and Other Plays.*
Find and write:

1　one sentence with an active verb

2　one sentence with a passive verb

The Pardoner's Viewpoint

A 1 Read the pardoner's speech from page 6 of *The Pardoner's Tale*.

I am a pardoner, this is my tale
It will make your teeth chatter, make you go pale
It may make you shiver with fear and dread
So leave the light on when you go to bed!

2 List the things the pardoner says will happen to the reader.

3 What sort of events does the reader expect
to happen in the play after reading this?

B 1 Read this speech by the pardoner from page 8.

But some people believed that a pardoner could forgive sins.
Some people would believe anything! Remember, it was six
hundred and fifty years ago, and people needed to hope for
better times. This was the time of the Black Death — the
Plague!

2 What exactly did the pardoner do for a living?

3 Do you think the pardoner really believed he could pardon
people? Which sentence tells you this?

4 Why did people believe the pardoner could forgive their sins?

Shakespeare's Language

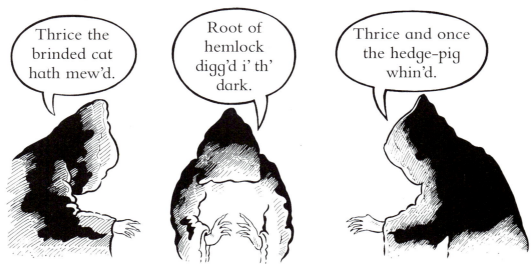

A 1 The word 'brinded' does not exist today. Can you find a word similar to it in a dictionary? Write down the word we use today and what it means.

2 Which word would we use today, instead of the word 'hath'?

3 Today we use a slightly different word for 'digg'd'. What is it?

> **Contractions are words in which letters are taken out and apostrophes are used in their place.**
> *e.g. they are — they're; they'd — they would*

B Copy out each witch's sentence writing the contractions as full words.

Spot the Word

A Find eighteen words from *The Scottish Play* in this word grid. List them under these headings:

nouns – people, places, objects or feelings, *e.g. witch*

adjectives – describe nouns, *e.g. scary witch*

verbs – action words, *e.g. ran, shouted*

adverbs – describe verbs, *e.g. chanted loudly*

S	T	A	G	E			M	O	V	I	N	G		
	W							I			O	L	D
		I						L					
			T					L					
				C				A	N	G	R	Y	
	L				H			G					T
H	O	R	R	I	B	L	E		E		T		R
	U								I			E
	D			A	C	T	O	R	U	M	B	L	E
	L				R							S
	Y				A			B	E	T	H	
	F	E	R	G	U	S			A		
				H				N		
		Q	U	I	C	K	L	Y		G	

B 1 Choose another play or story you have read and liked.

2 Draw a grid, 14 by 10 squares.

3 Fill the word grid, using nouns, adjectives, verbs and adverbs from the play or story.

44

Revolting Recipes!

A 1 Read aloud this witches' recipe from *The Scottish Play* with a partner.

2 Read the recipe again together in rhythm. Count four before you start. Clap each time you get to a word with a cross over it.

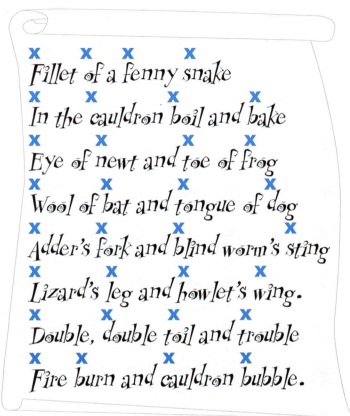

Fillet of a fenny snake
In the cauldron boil and bake
Eye of newt and toe of frog
Wool of bat and tongue of dog
Adder's fork and blind worm's sting
Lizard's leg and howlet's wing.
Double, double toil and trouble
Fire burn and cauldron bubble.

B Fill in the missing lines in this next made-up verse of the recipe using some of the rhyming words from the cauldron. Try to keep to the rhythm of the first verse, in section A. Try to use revolting ingredients.

Eye of cat and skin of snake

—————————————————

Dirt from feet and fur of bat

—————————————————

Smell of armpit, big toenail

—————————————————

rat hat shake
bake lake gnat
snail
quail tail

There/their/they're

> **There** means 'in that place'. *e.g. Mr Holmes is over there.*
> **Their** means 'connected to or belonging to them'.
> *e.g. It was their task to help Henrietta.*
> **They're** is a shortened form (contraction) of 'they are'.
> *e.g. They're going to Baskerville Hall.*

A Copy each sentence, filling in the gap with there, their or they're.

1 _____ is a knock at the door and Henrietta Baskerville enters Holmes' flat.

2 'I think _____ sure to find the prisoner,' replied Holmes.

3 In the earth of the flower bed, _____ were the footprints of a gigantic hound!

4 'Baskerville Hall has always been _____ family home,' Holmes told Watson.

B Work with a partner. You will each need a copy of *The Pardoner's Tale and Other Plays*. Look through the plays and find sentences with 'there', 'their', or 'they're' in them. One reads the sentences aloud and the other spells the 'there', 'their', or 'they're' word correctly.

Silent Movie

In a silent movie, characters act without speaking. In some silent movies, the characters act, then the screen goes blank and the words the characters would have said appear on the screen.

A You are going to plan a silent movie adaptation of the beginning of scene 3 of *The Curse of the Baskervilles*.

1 Re-read pages 56–57.

2 For each speech write:
   - who is speaking
   - what expression the character would have on his or her face
   - what they would be doing.

   e.g. Speech 1 Mr Stapleton – looking anxious and concerned – facing Henrietta and Dr Watson with hands out as if he would like to stop them going.

3 Write words which will appear on the screen to show what each character has just said. However, you will need to think carefully, because you cannot use more than nine words for each speech.

Detective Stories

A 1 Make a large copy of this spider diagram.

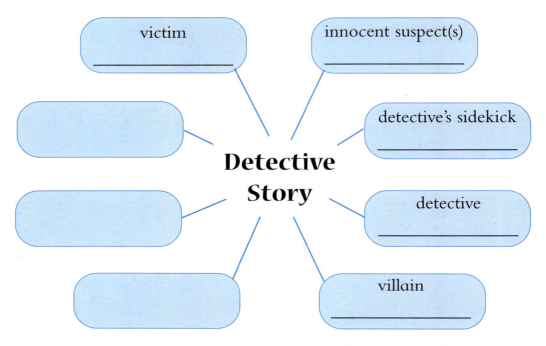

victim _____

innocent suspect(s) _____

detective's sidekick _____

Detective Story

detective _____

villain _____

2 Using the cast list at the beginning of *The Curse of the Baskervilles*, match each character with the role he or she plays. Write the names on your spider diagram.

3 Add these three headings to your spider diagram:
   crime – what happened
   motive – why the crime was committed
   setting – where the crime took place.

   Fill in the spaces under these headings for *The Curse of the Baskervilles* on your spider diagram.

B Plan your own detective story. Start by making another spider diagram, using the same eight headings, and fill in your ideas. Decide whether you want to set your detective story in the past, the present or the future.